BETH FLINTOFF

Beth is a playwright and theatre director. Writing includes *The Glove Thief, The World We Made* (Warwick Arts Centre), *Henry I of England, Matilda the Empress, Henry II* and *The Last Abbot* (all for Rabble), *The Rivals* (Watermill Theatre), *Who Killed Alfred Oliver?* (BBC Sounds & Rabble), *The Rebellious Women of Wimbledon* (Attic Theatre Company), *The True History of Susanna Shakespeare* (Bruntwood Prize longlist) and *Come to Where I'm From* (Paines Plough). She has collaborated twice as a writer/director with physical theatre ensemble Rhum and Clay, on *Jekyll and Hyde* and *Hardboiled: The Fall of Sam Shadow*, which toured with The Watermill before transferring to New Diorama in London. Beth also co-directed the multiple Off West End Award-winning play *The Incident Room* with David Byrne for New Diorama in 2019–20.

Beth is a member of the Sphinx Lab for British Female Playwrights 2020–21, a recipient of a 2021 MGCfutures Bursary, and an Associate Artist at Rabble Theatre Company, Reading.

Previously, she was the Outreach Director at The Watermill Theatre and she remains passionate about community theatre, working with young people, and increasing participation.

Beth Flintoff

THE BALLAD OF MARIA MARTEN

NICK HERN BOOKS
London
www.nickhernbooks.co.uk

A Nick Hern Book

The Ballad of Maria Marten first published in Great Britain in 2021 as a paperback original by Nick Hern Books Limited, The Glasshouse, 49a Goldhawk Road, London W12 8QP

Cover image: Rebecca Pitt

Designed and typeset by Nick Hern Books, London
Printed in the UK by Mimeo Ltd, Huntingdon, Cambridgeshire PE29 6XX

A CIP catalogue record for this book is available from the British Library

ISBN 978 1 83904 045 0

Introduction
Beth Flintoff

The murder of Maria Marten is a story that has been told and retold for the last two hundred years, with much lip-smacking enthusiasm for the gruesome details and unsubtle musings over whether or not she 'deserved it'. Here is the reversal of that telling. It's the story of Maria's murder, but it's an *un*-murdering.

There were many historical sources and studies to consult, but most useful was Peter Maggs' clear-headed account, *Murder in the Red Barn*. It was there I first learned that the barn was burnt down. It made me ask the question: what if the women that had loved Maria were not afraid, subdued or anxious, but were instead very, very angry? All the time I was writing, there was fire in my head.

On average, two women are killed by their partners every week in the UK. As part of my research, I spent time with an incredible group of women who have all experienced domestic violence or abuse. Their generosity, honesty and courage changed the direction of the writing. I decided to avoid all violence on stage and that we didn't need to meet the murderer at all – this is not a play about violence. It's a play about the people that experience it; it's a play about love.

I am indebted to Ivan Cutting for inviting me to tell this story, and the wonderful team at Eastern Angles; to Hal Chambers for his passionate, intelligent interpretation; to Luke Potter and Becca Randall for their stunning music and movement; to Matt Linley for believing in it; and to the wonderful actresses that have inhabited these characters on this journey: Lizzie, Sarah, Dani, Roxy, Emily, Lucy, Lydia, Bethan, Emma, Sue, Susie and Jess.

Music

Included in the text are the words to 'The Ballad of Maria
Marten' (which was sung during the 'un-murdering' at the start,
and then reprised later) and the 'Cherry Fair Song'. In any
future productions they could be used, or new lyrics could be
created, or there could be no singing at all. For the bawdy folk
number, we used 'The Lobster Song', an enjoyably frank
fourteenth-century rhyme that has been rewritten time and
again, and exists in multiple different versions.

Doubling

The play was originally performed by six women, doubling up
to play the men. It worked well, but all sorts of variations are
possible amongst the twelve characters. Feel free to explore
other options.

The Ballad of Maria Marten was commissioned by Ivan Cutting for Eastern Angles, and first performed by the company on the Ipswich Waterfront on 11 July 2018, with the following cast:

SARAH STOWE/LADY COOKE	Lydia Bakelmun
MARIA MARTEN	Elizabeth Crarer
ANN MARTEN	Sarah Goddard
LUCY BAALHAM/	
THOMAS CORDER	Lucy Grattan
THERESA HAVERS/	
PETER MATTHEWS	Bethan Nash
PHOEBE STOWE	Roxanne Palmer

It was subsequently produced by Eastern Angles and Matthew Linley Creative Projects, reopening at the Stephen Joseph Theatre, Scarborough, on 11 February 2020, with the following cast:

SARAH STOWE/LADY COOKE	Suzanne Ahmet
LUCY BAALHAM/	
THOMAS CORDER	Susie Barrett
MARIA MARTEN	Elizabeth Crarer
THERESA HAVERS/	
PETER MATTHEWS	Emma Denly
PHOEBE STOWE	Jessica Dives
ANN MARTEN	Sarah Goddard

Its third touring production opened at the Theatre Royal, Bury St Edmunds, on 16 September 2021, with the following cast and creative team:

SARAH STOWE/LADY COOKE	Lydia Bakelmun
LUCY BAALHAM/	
THOMAS CORDER	Susie Barrett
MARIA MARTEN	Elizabeth Crarer
PHOEBE STOWE	Jessica Dives
ANN MARTEN	Sarah Goddard
THERESA HAVERS	
/PETER MATTHEWS	Bethan Nash

Writer	Beth Flintoff
Director	Hal Chambers
Associate Director	Beth Flintoff
Designer	Verity Quinn
Music and Musical Direction	Luke Potter
Music Captain	Jess Dives
Lighting Designer	Zoe Spurr
Movement Direction	Rebecca Randall
Assistant Director	Becca Chadder
Movement Associate	Katie Albon
Producer	Matthew Linley
Company Stage Manager	Nikki Colclough
Stage Manager	Sarah Follon
Eastern Angles	
Company Stage Manager	Penny Griffin
Eastern Angles	
Production Manager	Steve Cooney
Set Construction	Dominic Eddington
Wardrobe	Faby Pym
Assistant Producer	Mitch Donaldson
Marketing	Emma Martin
Press	Chloé Nelkin Consulting
Artwork	Rebecca Pitt
Production Photography (2019)	Mike Kwasniak
Production Photography (2020)	Tony Bartholomew

With huge thanks to Dani McCallum, Emily Lloyd Saini, Ffion Lloyd, Julie Kearney, Ipswich High School, Ipswich School, Sudbury Quay Costume Hire, Susannah Rosenberg, Paula Pym, The Old Brewery Antiques, Amy Fisher, Paul Robinson, Julia Payne, Alyson Tipping, Helena Quarmby and Karen Goddard.

The Ballad of Maria Marten is an Eastern Angles and Matthew Linley Creative Projects co-production in association with the Stephen Joseph Theatre, Scarborough. The production is supported using public funding by the National Lottery through Arts Council England.

Eastern Angles is the regional touring company for the East of England producing over 120 shows with a sense of place in its nearly forty years' history. Principally based in Ipswich, at The Eastern Angles Centre with a satellite venue, The Undercroft, in Peterborough, it takes work to over sixty different venues each year. We mix rural touring into village halls with national tours and visits to the Edinburgh and London fringe; site-specific work, community plays and urban engagement in Peterborough all form part of our repertoire; care homes, schools, tithe barns and aircraft hangars feature amongst our venues.

Ipswich Office:
The Eastern Angles Centre
Gatacre Road
Ipswich
Suffolk IP1 2LQ

Peterborough Office:
Chauffeur's Cottage
St Peter's Road
Peterborough,
Cambridgeshire PE1 1YX

Admin: 01473 218202 | *Box Office:* 01473 211498
admin@easternangles.co.uk | www.easternangles.co.uk
Twitter: @easternangles | *Facebook:* /EasternAnglesTheatreCompany
Instagram: @easternangles | #MariaMarten

MATTHEW LINLEY
CREATIVE PROJECTS

MLCP's work tends to blur traditional boundaries often blending theatre, music, spoken word and the digital arts. Sometimes we work under our own steam, sometimes working with other production partners and venues

Recent work includes *The Chronicles of Atom and Luna* and *The Mystery of the Raddlesham Mumps* (with Funnelwick Limb), *The Ballad of Maria Marten* 2020 tour (with Eastern Angles) and the UK tour of *Nina: A Story About Me and Nina Simone* (with Unity Theatre/Riksteatern).

Together with Riksteatern (Sweden), MLCP have recently commissioned a new work from Anders Lustgarten for international touring in 2021/2022.

MLCP
Studio 118
37 Queen Street
Colchester CO1

www.matthewlinley.co.uk
Twitter: @matthewlinley
Facebook: /Matthew Linley Creative Projects

For the staff and survivors
at Lighthouse Women's Aid, Ipswich.

And for all the others who have been silenced.

Characters

MARIA MARTEN
PHOEBE STOWE
LUCY BAALHAM
THERESA HAVERS
SARAH STOWE
ANN MARTEN
LADY COOKE
THOMAS CORDER
PETER MATHEWS
MRS WOODSTOCK
MISS ANVIL
MISS PETTIGREW

In the original production, all the parts were played by six women.

Note on the Text

… indicates the character has run out of things to say

– indicates an interruption

/ indicates the point at which the next speaker interrupts

This text went to press before the end of rehearsals and so may differ slightly from the play as performed.

The Ballad of Maria Marten

Whenever I was lonely
There you were
You breathed my breath in for me
Took my air
I'm dreaming of a land afar
You bring me down to earth

You said that I had no one
Only you
You wanted me here with you
In the gloom
While I dreamed of a land afar
You sent me back to earth

You loved me so entirely
So you say
You couldn't bear to share me
Come what may
And banishing that land afar
You set me in the earth

ACT ONE

MARIA *steps forward. She looks a mess. She is dressed in men's clothes, which are torn and bloody. Her neck has a green handkerchief around it, under which you can just about make out strangle marks. She has an earring in one ear and the other ear is bloody.*

She is calm. She is not in any pain.

MARIA (*to the audience*). It's been a year since I died and still nobody has found me.

In the summer he ordered the workers to store wheat here, to cover up the loose stones.

No one questioned him. He's the master, now.

The wonderful thing about being dead is the exoneration. Right up until the end, I believed that all the things he told me were true: that I was full of sin, I seduced him, and I would go to hell. For a few months, I actually believed that I was going mad.

But the moment he bashed my brains out I was happy. For in my last moment of clarity I knew I was not mad. I had been tricked, and confused, but the fault lay with him.

The battle between good and evil is full of grey areas, but I think killing me with a spade puts him firmly on the devil's side.

She turns round. We can see that the back of her head has been bashed in: blood and brains mat her hair.

They do not know yet that I am dead, and I like that. I am not a murder victim, I am just a woman who has left the village.

Instead he dragged me into this barn, just across the field from our house. He shot me in the neck, strangled me with a handkerchief, and finally had a go with the spade. He was thorough.

I could tell you that story, but I don't want to yet. When they find my body, and see what he did to me, the last days of my life will be picked over like carrion, and I will belong to the world for comment.

But now, here, I can tell you who I really was. Before.

Music.

Enter SARAH, THERESA, PHOEBE, ANN *and* LUCY, *who start to gently clean her up. They clean away the blood and bruises. They help her into a new dress. They un-murder her. It might take a while; that's okay.*

The story begins where it ends: with girls playing with fire.

I was ten years old, working as a servant at the vicarage in a nearby village. Each morning I walked two miles to Layham through the woods.

One day I came across a girl about my age.

LUCY *is kneeling over a tinderbox.*

What are you doing?

LUCY. Starting a fire.

MARIA. Why?

LUCY. For practice.

MARIA. Don't you know how to do it?

LUCY. Yesterday I got it wrong.

MARIA. My mistress gets the boy to keep the fire going all night.

LUCY. I don't have a mistress, I have a *mother*.

She tries to strike the steel against the flint.

MARIA. You have to do it firmly, and then you have to breathe on it.

LUCY. I know that.

MARIA. Don't try so hard. It won't matter.

LUCY. You don't know my mother.

SARAH, THERESA *and* PHOEBE *approach.*

Uh-oh. That's Sarah Stowe and her cousin Phoebe, with their horrible friend. Don't worry, strange girl, I shall stand in front and protect you from their villainy.

PHOEBE. Hello, Maria! What are you up to?

LUCY. You know them?

MARIA. We're trying to start a fire because this girl has a horrible mother.

LUCY. No, I don't! Shhhh.

SARAH. Lucy Baalham? You're Constable Baalham's niece, ain't you?

LUCY. So what if I am? I can't help it.

SARAH. Your uncle had my father thrown in gaol because you reported him drunk.

LUCY. If you hurt me, God will see –

SARAH. What?

LUCY. Do whatever you want! I shall suffer in silence.

She closes her eyes and holds her hands out as if being crucified, and starts to pray under her breath –

The Lord is my shepherd, I shall not want, He maketh me down to lie – (*Trailing off.*) in green pastures…

She opens her eyes, one at a time.

SARAH. Just wanted to say thanks. My father's a right pain, we had the best night's sleep in months. Here.

She holds out a ribbon.

Been saving this for you.

LUCY. Mother don't like me to indulge in fripperies, because of God.

THERESA. Why don't God like ribbons?

LUCY. I'm not exactly sure. Something to do with Shame and Vanity.

THERESA. Sounds daft to me.

LUCY. Does it?

MARIA. Lucy, would you like to be in our club?

The others look at her, irritated.

THERESA. Maria – we have to vote on new members.

PHOEBE. Club is a bit full.

LUCY. What club?

MARIA. It's called the Hazard Club, where we do strange and dangerous things. Phoebe swallowed a frog once.

PHOEBE. Maria!

LUCY. I never heard of nothing like that.

MARIA. There's a Hazard Club in London where men have adventures – I heard them talking about it in the vicarage where I work. The Vicar said there was merriment and whoring.

LUCY. What *is* whoring?

THERESA. It's when men shout 'hooray' lots of times.

PHOEBE. We've tried it, and it's not as strange as swallowing a frog.

LUCY. Why do you want me to join?

THERESA. Yes, Maria, why do you want her to join?

MARIA. Because you're brave. And that's important.

LUCY. Am I?

PHOEBE. Is she?

MARIA. She is. That's going to be your Special Skill. Phoebe's is eating things. Sarah's is hitting the boys. Theresa's is holding her breath for a really long time under water.

LUCY. What's yours?

MARIA. Words.

SARAH. She can read.

LUCY. Properly?

SARAH. Every single word you ever saw.

MARIA. Vicar's wife instructed me in literature and elocution.

THERESA. That's why she sounds so la-di-da.

MARIA. Do you want to join our club?

LUCY. Yes please.

MARIA. Let's take a vote. Who else votes for Brave Lucy?

MARIA's hand is up in the air, SARAH's *too. Eventually* THERESA *and* PHOEBE *raise theirs.*

THERESA. But that's it, no more members. Otherwise it won't be a secret.

MARIA. It's just us, from now on.

They all put their hands together in a circle. LUCY, *after a slight hesitation, joins in.*

ALL. The Hazard Club!

MARIA. Now let's show her how to start a fire.

The GIRLS *crouch over the tinderbox.*

(*To the audience.*) In a place like Polstead, the boys go to school, if they're lucky. Sometimes we girls sat on the Village Green when it was sunny, and someone would try to teach us things. But for years, I was the only one that could read and write.

That was the year my mother died.

The GIRLS *gather around her.*

PHOEBE. Maria...

SARAH. We're sorry about your ma.

THERESA. What does it feel like?

LUCY. A relief, I expect.

They all look at her.

Or not – probably not a relief, no.

MARIA. Father hasn't spoken for a whole day. He sits on a bench outside the house and just looks at the garden.

PHOEBE. What happened?

MARIA. She died in the night. He woke up and there she was, lying next door to him. It's a bit –

It's a bit...

PHOEBE. Will you keep working at the vicarage?

MARIA. No, I'm coming home to look after Ninny and the baby.

SARAH. We bought you a hanky. Theresa tried to sew your name on it.

SARAH presents a green handkerchief. The word 'MARRYA' has been stitched on.

THERESA. Did I get it right?

MARIA. Yeah.

The GIRLS go and MARIA is left alone.

A new life swallowed me. I was a ten-year-old mother. Up before dawn, getting the house ready, and then working all day long until Father came home. I did the work of three servants.

Until one Sunday, when I came home from church, and there was someone in the kitchen.

ANN steps forward.

Who are you?

ANN. Oh – heavens – she's here! I never dreamed of you coming back so fast – you must walk everso fast? And here's me trying to sort things out still. I wanted everything perfect for when you got back so's you could just put your feet up and your pa could just sit with his pipe – he does smoke a pipe? – I was thinking he probably does but I forgot and then I felt too silly to ask.

MARIA. Sorry – Miss – ?

ANN. Hah! She calls me Miss! Not likely! It's Ann, or Annie.
They used to call me Nitbin at Manor Farm, on account of
the number of times I got nits, but if it's all the same to you
I'd like to put that name behind me.

MARIA. If you have come to take tea with my father you are
extremely welcome, but you must not make it, that is my job.

A beat.

ANN. I *love* you. He said I would and I do.

*Unexpectedly she starts to cry, fanning herself energetically
with one hand.*

Sorry. It's just. What are you, eleven? I mean when I was
eleven I was just this skinny little wild thing straight out the
orphanage, scrubbing floors, and look at you – you're so
neat. The pride and joy of your father! The hope that nestles
in the innocent breast! And now I'm here, at last.

Maria Marten: *I am your mother!*

MARIA. No... She died about a year ago.

ANN. I've come to take care of your beautiful innocent soul.
I'm to be your father's new wife.

MARIA. Father is marrying *you*?

ANN. I know, it's astonishing, I never dreamt of it neither. Such
a handsome man with the best pair of boots this side of
Sudbury, and he chose me – I shall spend the rest of my life
working out why.

MARIA. Why didn't he tell me?

ANN. Well it's true, he's not much of a talker, your pa, but I can
manage that for both of us. I 'spect he thought it was best left
until everything was sorted.

MARIA. I need to go and talk to my father.

ANN. Look it's alright, when you imagined a new mother I
don't suppose you thought it'd be a little bit of scrag like me.
I might be useful, though, sometimes, on account of being a
dairy maid for five years – I can milk fifteen cows in one day
and scrub a floor so clean you can see your face in it. And on

account of all the milking, I'm superb at sitting on stools so you'll never have to buy me a chair.

I mean, the price of furniture, these days. It's just a disgrace.

MARIA *nods and starts to go* –

Thing is, if you tell your pa you don't like me, he'll call it all off. He adores you that much. So you can, you know... do that, if you want.

But I'd like to stay. I heard how much you do for him – how you get up at four in the morning and make the breakfast. It might be nice for you to have someone else do it too.

A beat.

MARIA. Alright.

ANN. Alright? You mean – yes?

MARIA. Yes –

ANN. Oh. Oh. (*Starts crying again.*) This is the happiest day of my life.

MARIA. Welcome to our home, Ann.

ANN. I never had a home.

MARIA. Let's make tea, shall we?

ANN *backs away.*

From that day, I began to have a childhood. These were the happy years. When summer meant picking cherries, and reading on the bench in the garden, and running up to the top of the lane to meet my friends for wild and secret activities with the Hazard Club.

PHOEBE *runs in backwards.*

PHOEBE. Maria! Today we're only allowed to walk backwards.

MARIA. Why?

PHOEBE. Theresa's put a curse on anyone who walks forwards in Polstead. I just came to tell you in case you dropped dead because you didn't know. I fell over twice but I didn't care because you're my best friend in the whole world and I wanted to save your life.

MARIA. You are the best friend ever, Phoebe Stowe.

PHOEBE. Yeah, I know, I actually think I would die for you.

MARIA. No I would die for *you*.

They hug passionately. PHOEBE *reverses back out again.*

The Club was banned by our parents when Theresa accidentally turned her hair blue. Questions were asked about the nature of our activities. It turned out that Sarah had kissed a boy for a dare, found she liked it, and was now going to have his baby.

In short, rather to our surprise, we suddenly discovered that we were women.

The GIRLS *change their clothes and hair so that they look older. They sing a bawdy folk song, after which they all laugh, except* LUCY, *who's a bit shocked. The baby cries.* SARAH *goes to it.*

LUCY. That is an absolutely disgusting song.

SARAH. God's life this baby is obsessed with my tits.

LUCY. Don't swear, God will hear you.

SARAH. I'd like to think He's concentrating on other things, like the price of bread.

THERESA. I've got apples, if you want?

She starts to hand them around.

PHOEBE. Where'd you get these?

THERESA. Bandy Jim has fallen desperately in love with me, even though he's about sixty-five. I told him I love Jonnie Pryke to distraction, like a madness, but fruit helps me think more clearly.

LUCY. Theresa Havers, that is almost prostitution.

SARAH. I actually *did it* with Eddie Living in exchange for a sausage roll. That *was* prostitution.

THERESA (*to* SARAH). I've been meaning to ask. That method of not having a baby, that you swore by with so much confidence?

SARAH. Flushing your bits with cold rainwater.

LUCY. I think we can safely say it don't work.

THERESA. Because I saw something in a magazine. I think it's an advert for a *device*.

She hands a torn-out page to MARIA.

MARIA (*reading*). 'Cup-Shaped Ladies' Silk Sponge, two shillings.'

They all gather round to stare at it. Simultaneously their heads all tilt to one side as they try to work out what it is.

PHOEBE. Does that go where I think it's meant to go?

SARAH. All the way in.

MARIA. What's the string for?

SARAH. To pull it back out afterwards, so you can use it again.

They all wince.

THERESA. I'm thinking it's not a bad price.

LUCY (*pointing at* SARAH). Is the sight of this miserable woman and her bastard child, the product of illicit lust and dangerous promiscuity, really no deterrent?

SARAH. Hey! I'm not miserable.

THERESA. I want to marry John but we can't until I'm eighteen, my pa won't allow it.

LUCY. A modest woman submits to her husband's embraces to gratify him, not for her own desires.

SARAH. Bleeeuuurghghh.

MARIA. Thomas Corder tried to kiss me yesterday, behind the Red Barn.

ALL. No!

SARAH. Course he did. All farmers' sons are randy.

PHOEBE. What did you do?

MARIA. Told him no, of course. He makes me feel queasy.

THERESA. But they rent all the fields this side of the village.

MARIA. I don't want a field. He can barely hold a conversation.

SARAH. And the dandruff.

THERESA. Least he don't go out and get drunk.

PHOEBE. It don't matter, if she don't like him, that's that.

MARIA. Thing is, money's tight at home. I mean, really tight.

LUCY. Maria, the richest treasure a woman can possess is her virtue.

SARAH. Balls. I'd rather have a decent vegetable patch.

MARIA. We have a house full of children, and since the harvest failed my father has been laid off.

They all stare at her for a moment. THERESA *offers her another apple.* PHOEBE *puts her arm round her sympathetically.*

We could not buy new clothes that year.

The GIRLS *make* MARIA*'s clothing look bedraggled and tattered. Then they leave her.*

We started to run out of food in the autumn. Soon the hunger was a constant noise in our heads.

The Martens' cottage.

Step forward ANN, *holding a baby, which is crying.*

ANN. He's got an awful flush.

MARIA. It's just a cold.

ANN. Your pa's working for the Corders for the next few weeks. If we can just hold out till his pay comes in...

MARIA. We should never have sold the pig.

ANN. What about dinner?

MARIA. I'll try and catch a rabbit.

ANN. This is worse than the workhouse. Tell me something good, Maria, or I might just expire right here in front of the stove.

MARIA. Have some beer.

ANN. It's the last of all we have.

MARIA. It's alright, you need it.

MARIA pours the final dregs of the beer and hands it to ANN.

Once it's gone, it's gone.

ANN is about to drink, but there's a knock. She looks through the window.

ANN. It's Thomas Corder!

Enter THOMAS CORDER.

THOMAS. M – Mrs Marten?

ANN. Master Thomas!

THOMAS. I – er – hope I don't disturb you.

ANN. Not at all.

THOMAS. I've been in Stoke-by-Nayland – I hoped to catch your husband on my way home. If...

ANN. He's still in the top field. He'll be home any moment – you can wait in the kitchen.

THOMAS. Thank you. It's a cold day.

A tiny hesitation, in which ANN struggles with the fact that she has nothing to offer him. Eventually –

ANN. Can I get you a mug of beer, Master Thomas?

THOMAS. Well – I won't say no – thank you, Mrs Marten.

She hands him the last of the beer.

He downs it in one go.

They watch him. He exhales with satisfaction.

Ah. That's good, that is. I've had a hard day, and no mistake, Mrs Marten.

ANN. Sorry to hear it.

THOMAS. In truth – rather than trouble you more, I could perhaps just leave a message?

ANN. Course.

THOMAS. It's about the work your husband was going to do – we won't be needing him after all.

ANN. You won't?

THOMAS. Turns out my father had already engaged a couple of other fellows, so we'd have too many, you see. It won't inconvenience you, though?

ANN. Well – we were relying on the money.

THOMAS. I'll put in a good word at High Trees Farm, if you like?

MARIA. Ann. I can hear little Ambrose calling for you upstairs.

ANN *looks at her in surprise.*

Probably bumped his head again – I'll see Master Thomas out.

ANN. Oh – will you excuse me?

THOMAS. Of course.

ANN *exits.*

MARIA. How are you, Thomas?

THOMAS (*stiffly*). Well, thank you, Miss Marten.

MARIA. I thought we were friends.

THOMAS. I feel bad about your father. It was our mistake, not his.

MARIA. Can't you give him work doing something else? He's the best mole-catcher in the district.

THOMAS. We don't have any moles –

MARIA. I saw a streak of molehills in one of the north fields this morning.

THOMAS. Did you?

MARIA. About the other day, when you tried to kiss me. I liked it.

THOMAS. You didn't give that impression.

MARIA. Didn't I?

THOMAS. You hit me rather hard across the face.

MARIA. Isn't that what women are supposed to do when young men surprise them?

THOMAS. It's news to me.

MARIA. You can try it again, if you like.

Awkwardly, he moves towards her.

Only, promise me one thing?

THOMAS. What?

MARIA. The moles. Give the job to my father.

THOMAS. Look – we can't afford to just give out work. It's been a bad harvest –

MARIA. Alright – let me do it. You won't need to pay me as much, right?

She kisses him. It's awkward and clunky.

She pretends to love it.

Then he backs away.

MARIA *is left alone.*

I stood with my father in the field for a week while he caught moles, and we all pretended I had done it. Then they paid me half of what they would have paid him.

A week later there were no more moles.

I would go to the Corders' farmhouse in the evenings and meet Thomas Corder in the dairy. In this way I ensured us a steady supply of milk and cheese.

There were good days, when I tried to like him and almost succeeded. And bad days, when our love was a quiet tug-of-war.

THOMAS *holds out a loaf of bread for* MARIA. *She goes to take it. He snatches it away, he won't give it until she gives him a kiss. She does so. He hands over the bread and she tears a bit off.*

THOMAS *backs away.*

MARIA *eats some of the bread and hands the rest to* ANN.

ANN. D'you like him, then?

Cos we'll manage some other way, if –

MARIA. Don't wait up for me tonight.

ANN. Maria, I don't think God would want you to... *you know...* for the sake of some food. It says in the Bible that the heavens will provide.

MARIA. Just don't tell Father.

ANN. Oh, Lordy.

ANN *backs away.* THERESA *comes towards* MARIA.

MARIA. Did you get it? The 'device'?

THERESA. It hasn't arrived.

MARIA. But you sent the money weeks ago.

THERESA. Sarah says we've been robbed. Apparently it happens all the time.

MARIA. I don't know how much longer I can hold him off. He's getting very enthusiastic.

THERESA. You'll have to do the flushing thing.

MARIA. What if it doesn't work?

THERESA. Make sure the water's really cold, and do it straight away. Maybe you could jiggle up and down a bit?

MARIA. Jiggle up and / down!

THERESA. I can't think of anything else. Good luck.

THERESA goes.

MARIA. My first time was rushed, and heavy, up against the wall in the Corder's farmhouse kitchen. Afterwards, I jumped vigorously up and down, which astonished him very much.

She looks about her for a moment.

We did it here once, in this very barn that I'm buried in. Did you know that?

I used to like coming here when I was alive. The way the daylight creeps in through broken slats. The warmth of hay bales and the sound of chickens outside.

In the summer evenings it has a red hue that people think is ghostly, but I know is just a trick of the light.

It's a peaceful place to wait, until I am discovered.

Enter ANN, suddenly. She is wearing her night things, with a cloak thrown about her shoulders. Her hair is loose.

ANN. Maria!

She looks around her, without seeing MARIA.

Maria!

MARIA. Ann...

ANN. Are you here? Maria!

Enter PHOEBE.

PHOEBE. Ann – what is it? – we can hear you way across the field –

ANN. I saw her.

PHOEBE. Here? – In the barn?

ANN. I don't know –

PHOEBE. You saw her here?

ANN. I'm not sure – I just – I –

PHOEBE. For God's sake, where?

ANN. In my dream.

I had a dream.

PHOEBE *breathes out in frustration. She sinks onto a hay bale.*

ANN *sits next to her.*

I'm sorry.

It just – it seemed so… I saw her.

PHOEBE. You gave me a fright.

ANN. Have you given up?

PHOEBE. On what?

ANN. Nobody talks about her any more.

PHOEBE. When she's ready, she'll write to us –

ANN. When she's *ready* – ?

PHOEBE. – and tell us what she's been up to.

ANN. What if he's lying? She's hurt somewhere, or he's keeping her by force…?

PHOEBE. Don't think horrible thoughts.

ANN. Is it though? Is it more horrible?

The thought that she would just go to the Isle of Wight – wherever that is! – and secretly get married, and never write to me – that she would just leave us – and her little boy behind... That's the worst possible thought.

I mean, does the Isle of Wight even exist?

PHOEBE. Yeah, it does.

ANN. I dreamt she was in here. It felt very real to me.

She stands up.

But I s'pose it weren't real, were it? Just me being stupid, again.

She goes.

PHOEBE. Annie...

She looks around her, as if she's trying to imagine that MARIA *is there.*

Hello?

MARIA *approaches, longing to touch her.*

Then PHOEBE *goes.*

MARIA *is left alone.*

MARIA. By the time Christmas came, and I could bring things to an end with Thomas Corder, it was already too late. One day I was alone at home when I had a visitor.

Enter LADY COOKE.

LADY COOKE. Miss Marten? Ah – good – you're in! Maria, isn't it?

MARIA. Lady Cooke! How do you do? (*She bobs a curtsy.*)

LADY COOKE. Good gracious. The state of this cottage.

MARIA. We do our best to keep it clean, ma'am, only –

LADY COOKE. Bless you – it's clean as a whistle – I mean the cold, my dear! And you have no carpets!

MARIA. No.

LADY COOKE. I'm sure there used to be carpets in this house. I have some floor rugs I do not need, I shall send them over from the Hall. No, no – don't offer me anything – here is a basket for your stepmother.

MARIA. Oh – there's no need –

LADY COOKE. It's alright, my dear, the second Thursday of the month is my day for Visiting the Poor.

MARIA. We manage perfectly fine, thank you, ma'am.

LADY COOKE. Doesn't look like it. Anyway I came because I needed to ask. Is it true?

MARIA. What?

LADY COOKE. That you are expecting a child and the father is Thomas Corder, the son of our tenant?

A beat.

MARIA. Yes, ma'am, it is true.

LADY COOKE. You do not seem ashamed.

MARIA. I believe the blame should be equally shared between the man and the woman, ma'am.

LADY COOKE. Why on earth should you think that? Have you been reading?

MARIA. Well – sometimes –

LADY COOKE. When will you marry?

MARIA. He hasn't asked.

LADY COOKE. He must. He must ask today.

MARIA. His mother does not approve.

LADY COOKE. Why? Is there something wrong with you?

MARIA. No, ma'am, I don't think so.

LADY COOKE. You attend church. Your father does not drink. You speak well and are not unattractive. What can be his mother's objection?

MARIA. We are not the same station in life.

LADY COOKE. Nonsense – who do they think they are? –
they're not *gentry*.

MARIA. I was going to go to the magistrate, ma'am, for a
bastardy order when the child is born, so that I'd get
support –

LADY COOKE. Don't go. You cannot bring up a child in this
village and the father live just around the corner, I won't
have it. Leave it with me, my dear: I like you. Who cares
about station? Love will have its way!

MARIA. Thank you.

LADY COOKE. You will make a charming couple. What do
you read, by the way? Keats?

MARIA. Conduct books, mainly, ma'am. Advice to women on
how to be a good Christian.

LADY COOKE. You're pulling my leg. Are you? Please say
you are.

MARIA. Yes, ma'am. I am very fond of Keats.

LADY COOKE. Hah! You are quite something, I do declare!
Well, I must dash. The refurbishment of the living quarters at
the Hall is completely exhausting. What is it with builders?
They seem to think one can live without drawing rooms for
months on end.

She goes.

MARIA. She did as she said. We made plans. Thomas said he
would marry me once the baby was born.

Enter THERESA, PHOEBE *and* LUCY. *They give* MARIA
a pregnancy 'bump'.

PHOEBE. D'you like him more now?

MARIA. The house helps. Enough food to go around.

PHOEBE. But you'll be married to *him*.

LADY COOKE *steps forward again, brandishing a book.*

LADY COOKE. Hullooo! Miss Marten!

LUCY. It's Lady Cooke!

The GIRLS *all curtsy respectfully.*

LADY COOKE. Oh, look, you're entertaining half the females in the village. How jolly! I was on my way past in the carriage and thought I'd drop off this. Something to look at during your confinement.

MARIA (*taking the book*). *Pride and Prejudice*?

LADY COOKE. Some parts are better than others. Anyway, must dash – we're off to the opening of a brand-new theatre in Bury St Edmunds. Rather exciting.

LADY COOKE *goes.*

MARIA. I don't know why she took such an interest in me. But thanks to her we survived the winter and the baby came at the end of the spring.

Suddenly, MARIA *is fragile. The* GIRLS *help her out of her pregnancy bump, and take her gently away.*

ANN *and* LADY COOKE *step forward.*

LADY COOKE. Mrs Marten? Hulloooo!

ANN. Lady Cooke! How nice –

LADY COOKE. I have come to check on the patient. Patients.

ANN. It's very kind / of you –

LADY COOKE. Don't mention it. It's the second Thursday of the month, et cetera.

ANN. Is it?

LADY COOKE. Well, let's pretend it is. I bear gifts: soap, a counterpane for the baby – I thought you might need more linen, was I right? Milk for the –

ANN. Lady Cooke. The baby died.

A beat.

LADY COOKE. Oh dear.

How very unfortunate.

ANN. I know some people might say it's for the best.

LADY COOKE. They're probably right – nevertheless, what a profoundly horrible thing to say.

Will she still marry the Corder boy, do you think?

ANN. He has not been to visit.

LADY COOKE. Since when?

ANN. Since the spring, my lady.

LADY COOKE. He never saw the child?

ANN. Not once.

LADY COOKE. Pfff. So much for love. How does Maria?

ANN. Her father says she will mend.

LADY COOKE. Quite right. They generally do.

ANN. It just seems like a very sad thing, to see her crying so much. She never used to cry. Whereas I cry quite often, so it wouldn't be so odd.

LADY COOKE (*a sudden idea*). When she is back to normal, in a month or two, send her to the Hall, would you?

ANN. The Hall?

LADY COOKE. I have a thought for how to cheer her up. Have you got a bath?

ANN. No. But we could borrow one…

LADY COOKE. Tell her to have a bath, and then come. Cheerio!

MARIA. A few months later, bathed, with fear and trembling, I set foot in Polstead Hall.

MARIA *steps forward to become a human mannequin. The company remove* MARIA*'s outer dress, revealing just a smock underneath.* LADY COOKE *watches with amusement while a dressmaker,* MRS WOODSTOCK, *dresses* MARIA, *talking as she does so.* MISS PETTIGREW *and* MISS ANVIL *watch too, murmuring words of admiration.*

MRS WOODSTOCK. And here we have an outfit perfect for taking a walk in the early-summer evenings. I call the colour 'marshmallow blossom' – fastened down the front with three large wrought buttons. A double gold chain with a watch – should you choose to wear one – I like a watch…

MISS ANVIL. Me too!

MISS PETTIGREW. Oh, I *adore* a watch.

MRS WOODSTOCK. The look is completed with black kid half-boots and yellow gloves.

MISS ANVIL. Oh, she looks a picture!

LADY COOKE. Doesn't she?

MISS ANVIL. The neatness of her figure!

MISS PETTIGREW. Such a charming outfit. I shall buy the pelisse this instant, Mrs Woodstock.

MRS WOODSTOCK. Very good, madam.

LADY COOKE. What do you think, Maria? There is a looking glass over there.

MARIA *goes to look. She stares at her reflection.*

MARIA. I don't recognise myself.

MISS ANVIL. Is it not what you would normally wear, Miss Marten?

LADY COOKE. Miss Marten's normal attire is rather more prosaic.

MISS ANVIL. I suppose it must get muddy sometimes out here.

MARIA. It wouldn't be very practical for feeding the pigs.

A moment of stunned silence. Then they burst out laughing.

MISS PETTIGREW. I say – what a hoot!

MISS ANVIL. I nearly died of shock!

MISS PETTIGREW. Miss Marten, won't you let us do your hair for you?

MISS ANVIL. Oh, do let's!

MARIA. If you like.

They sit her down and start to arrange her hair.

Music.

The feeling of their soft hands on my hair. The rustle of silk next to my skin. The way they talk – not about laundry or baking or feeding the chickens – but about ballet and books and music.

They're so clean. Their smell.

The last time I was touched was with a pair of forceps. But they're touching me like I'm precious.

Step forward PETER MATHEWS. *He watches her for a while – he is smitten from the start.*

Then the ladies back away, ushered off by LADY COOKE, *leaving* MARIA *alone. She is lost in a world of comfort, overwhelmed by it.*

PETER *clears his throat –* MARIA *jumps.*

PETER. I'm sorry to disturb you.

MARIA. No... Sorry –

PETER. I was looking for my sister, Lady Cooke. She's not expecting me, I'm afraid I have turned up at her door like the prodigal brother I am. You must be one of her friends?

MARIA. No – not really – I'm Maria Marten from the village. (*She bobs a curtsy.*)

PETER. Oh, no – please –

MARIA. I'm just the model for the clothes. I mean, I don't normally look like this.

PETER. How do you normally look?

MARIA. A bit of a mess, if I'm honest. I hadn't realised just how much of a mess, until today.

PETER. I should have thought you look very fine no matter what.

A beat.

MARIA. I must get changed. I'll be needed back home.

PETER. May I assist you – do you have far to go?

MARIA. Oh no – thank you – it's only round the corner.

PETER. It's pouring with rain, though – have you an umbrella?

MARIA. I must have forgotten it.

PETER. Let me lend you one of ours. Here –

He fetches a green umbrella.

This should keep the worst at bay.

She takes the umbrella.

MARIA. Thank you.

PETER. Peter Mathews.

MARIA. Thank you, Mr Mathews. I'll bring it back.

PETER. Lovely. No rush.

PETER *backs away.*

The company put MARIA *back into her everyday clothes.*

MARIA. There is a world out there of manners and gentility and not getting wet in the rain. There is a world with time to curl hair and worry about lace veils. With walks and conversation and roast pork on Sunday.

What separates us? My life is so utterly opposite to theirs – why?

I wanted it – I wanted to see Mr Mathews every day, and I wanted Lady Cooke to love me like a sister. And I really wanted to keep the green umbrella.

She puts it up.

It rains.

She enjoys walking through Polstead in the rain. SARAH,
PHOEBE, THERESA *and* LUCY *gather around her.*

PHOEBE. Maria! Where'd you get that?

MARIA. It's a loan from a gentleman.

PHOEBE. What gentleman?

MARIA. They don't get wet in the rain. They don't even know
what mud is.

SARAH. She's gone mad.

MARIA. Come under!

All five GIRLS *huddle under the umbrella. It's a bit cramped.*

PHOEBE. Where've you been?

MARIA. I met some rich folks and decided to marry one of
them.

SARAH. We're not good enough now, girls.

MARIA. You can all come round for tea once a week.

PHOEBE. Who is he?

MARIA. He's called Peter Mathews, and he's staying at the
Hall. He's half in love with me already, I just need to work
on the other half.

THERESA. You could pretend to faint in church?

PHOEBE. Or pinch your cheeks so you look like you're
blushing?

SARAH. No, no, no, lean over and hitch up your bosoms so
they tilt right in towards his face, and then, with your
tongue –

LUCY. Sarah Stowe! Stop leading her astray.

SARAH. Oh, don't be boring, it's life.

LUCY. I prefer boring to your current condition. Anyone can
tell you're pregnant again.

They all look at SARAH *in surprise.*

PHOEBE. Are you?

SARAH. I'm quite pleased actually – it'll be nice for Charlie.

THERESA. Who's the father this time?

SARAH. Your John. Joking! I'm not sure, there's a few possibilities.

LUCY. Reverend Whitmore is not going to be pleased with you.

SARAH. Probably not, he's one of them.

They all really gasp. She chuckles.

You lot are so gullible.

MARIA. I hope it lives.

A beat.

SARAH. Me too.

A beat.

PHOEBE. I've got it! You need to dance with Peter Mathews at the Cherry Fair. Your finest dress, music, the sunset –

THERESA. Oh, that's good, that's very good.

MARIA. The Cherry Fair?

THERESA. He don't stand a chance.

PHOEBE. He'll be yours by nightfall.

THERESA. You're gonna get married to a gentleman.

SARAH. And we'll all come round for tea.

A beat while they all consider this.

THERESA. I'm getting a very wet arse.

The GIRLS *back away.*

MARIA *folds the umbrella down. She strokes it gently.*

MARIA. This umbrella was the first thing I was hit with. That wasn't what killed me, though. Umbrellas are pointy, but not so lethal as a spade.

16th July 1822. The Polstead Cherry Fair.

Music. The company gather around MARIA, *singing a song.*

During the song, they tidy MARIA *up a bit, and put flowers in her hair.*

The ensemble creates the sense of the fair: there's a lot of cherry-selling, of course – cherries, cherry pies, cherry brandy. Also sales of other fruit and veg, bacon and dairy stalls. This is the major annual event of the village.

'Cherry Fair Song'.

ENSEMBLE.
> My true love has gone to the fair,
> Lord knows what he plans to do there,
> He's gone for the cherries,
> To drink himself merry,
> My true love has gone to the fair.
>
> *Oh the music is dancing*
> *And eyes are a-glancing*
> *For love is so sweet in the air.*
> *You always find love at the fair!*
>
> My true love has gone to the fair
> He says he will meet with me there
> To kiss me unbidden
> And buy me a ribbon
> To put in my copper-brown hair.
>
> *Oh the music is dancing*
> *And eyes are a-glancing*
> *For love is so sweet in the air.*
> *You always find love at the fair!*
>
> Her true love he went to the fair
> And she went a-meeting him there
> And then five years later
> They're wed and he'll hate 'er
> And they'll put it down to the fair.
> Oh, it's all because of the fair.

Oh the music is dancing
And eyes are a-glancing
For love is so sweet in the air.
You always find love at the fair!

PETER *is there.* MARIA *watches him.*

MARIA. It's a fine thing, to fall in love before you die, especially if you die young. I fell in love with Peter Mathews at the Cherry Fair. I had to endure Thomas Corder first, though.

THOMAS *approaches.*

THOMAS. Maria. Hello. I've been um... looking for you.

MARIA. I live in the same house I always did, Thomas.

THOMAS. Perhaps we could... I mean – later –

MARIA. We could what?

THOMAS. Have a dance?

MARIA. Am I being tested for lunacy?

THOMAS. No. I'm sorry, I just –

MARIA. I am already engaged to dance with another gentleman. So, no, I cannot dance with you.

THOMAS. A gentleman? Who?

MARIA. If you must know, Mr Mathews.

THOMAS. Lady Cooke's brother? He has an income of five hundred a year!

MARIA. Well, he and I are friends.

THOMAS. Mr Mathews! Over here!

MARIA. No – don't call him over –

PETER *approaches.*

PETER. Corder! Good to see you!

THOMAS. Mr Mathews, it's – I – wanted to say, thank you, sir.

It's good of you to agree to dance with Miss Marten. She's had some trouble lately, and there's talk in the village. To be honest, the blame should be at least partly on my side, sir.

PETER (*confused, but trying to play along*). I am always delighted to help.

THOMAS. Well – thank you for taking her on.

MARIA (*with barely suppressed rage*). Oh, yes. You are both all kindness.

A beat.

PETER. Miss Marten – may I hold you to your promise of a dance?

MARIA. No, thank you, I shall dance on my own.

They back away. The music starts up again and she dances on her own. It's a bit sad at first, and awkward. But gradually it becomes alright, and a bit funny.

PHOEBE *joins in, and* MARIA *is boosted by the support.*

In time, ANN *also starts to dance with them, and then all the* GIRLS *join in.*

They dance, laughing and breathless. There is, for a moment, pure joy in it.

PETER *watches.*

Eventually, they beckon him to join in, and he does. Gradually the others peel away, and MARIA *and* PETER *are left dancing alone.*

The world slows around them and the sun sets over the end of the Cherry Fair, as PETER *and* MARIA *dance.*

PETER. This is glorious. I had no idea.

MARIA. Of what?

PETER. That this is what happens at a fair.

MARIA. You've never been?

PETER. I live in London.

MARIA. I'd love to go to London.

PETER. No, it's horrible, I'm never going back. I'm going to stay in Polstead and organise a fair once a week.

MARIA. We might get bored?

PETER. I will never get bored of this. It's...

MARIA. Glorious?

PETER. Yes! That's exactly what it is. You're a mind-reader!

The GIRLS, *watching, give* MARIA *a thumbs-up sign. They back away, giggling.*

MARIA. Not only did I fall in love before I died, but I have good reason to believe that he loved me in return, and there is much to be said for that. We had many months of actual, real happiness.

One day – one *glorious* day, he arrived outside our cottage in a carriage.

PETER *arrives in a carriage and* MARIA *jumps in.*

ANN. Oh, my giddy aunt! Maria, where are you going?

MARIA. Annie, we're going to see the *sea*!

PETER. I shall return her tomorrow, safe and sound, I promise, Mrs Marten.

Harwich. Seagulls fly overhead and the sea is a gentle roar.

MARIA. How many millions of people do you think there are, all around the world, connected by the ocean? We're just a speck.

PETER. Millions of tiny specks – and not one of them as marvellous as you. I think I'm the luckiest chap in England.

MARIA. Thank you for bringing me here.

PETER. My father knows.

She turns to stare at him.

My sister told him. She thought she was being kind.

MARIA. What did he say?

PETER. He wept.

MARIA. Oh.

PETER. When we were children he beat us all the time, my brothers and I, and we used to think it was terrible. Now I know that crying is worse.

MARIA. I'm not good enough for his son.

PETER. If he could only meet you – see what I see. We must be patient, and bide our time, and he will come round.

MARIA. What if he doesn't?

PETER. I'll think of something.

I want to marry you.

A beat.

Is that – alright?

MARIA. It's a bloody miracle.

They embrace.

PETER. I have booked rooms at an inn nearby. But we can go home any time you want.

MARIA. Separate rooms?

PETER. Yes, of course.

MARIA. Cancel one. Tell them I am your wife.

PETER. Maria. You don't have to –

MARIA. I never travelled further than Hadleigh. Even my father has to go to Ipswich once a month, but he never takes us. You don't understand what it's like to be a woman, Peter, and never be needed anywhere except the kitchen.

PETER. But what if you –

MARIA. I want to be your wife, and to have children with you, and never be apart from you, and to go wherever you go, and to finally mean something.

PETER. You do. Mean something. You do.

PETER *backs away;* MARIA *picks up a bucket as* ANN *comes forward.*

ANN. Maria. I'm sorry, but I have to ask. What are you doing?

MARIA. Feeding the chickens.

ANN. With Peter Mathews. I mean, I think it's marvellous that you're in love and all, but he's a very, very rich man, and it's a little bit frightening.

MARIA. Did Father put you up to this?

ANN. I told him I'd be no good at explaining.

MARIA. Ann, love does not know a person's wealth.

ANN. Everyone's talking about it – (*As* MARIA *starts to go.*) Where are you off to now?

MARIA. Gleaning in the field to the west of Flemings Lane. I'll be back at sunset.

ANN. They joke about it in the pub. It's making life hard for your father.

MARIA (*stopping and turning back*). It makes his life hard? Because of *talk*?

ANN. A man does not like to have to –

MARIA. Who bought him a new pair of boots last month?

ANN. It seems like a high price, though, don't it?

MARIA. I learnt to do this with Thomas Corder, and you never stopped me. I learnt my price then, when we were starving – and that price was three days' work, a few loaves of bread and some cheese. Now we are not starving, and I am with a man who makes my heart happy, and everyone is concerned about my soul. He gives us things because he loves me.

ANN. But the gossip in the village –

MARIA. What other people think of me is none of my business. Father might consider not going to the pub. He could stay at home and sew buttons on his own shirt.

Now please excuse me, I have high hopes of a good three bushels of wheat today.

She begins to put on a rather beautiful straw hat with ribbons. It looks incongruous with her simple dress.

ANN. In that hat?

MARIA. Yes, in this hat! And I'm taking my umbrella!

She picks up the green umbrella.

ANN *backs away.*

LADY COOKE *steps forward.*

LADY COOKE. Thank you for coming, Maria.

I'm afraid I must ask you to stop seeing my brother.

A beat.

MARIA. Lady Cooke –

LADY COOKE. Everybody knows. The whole of Polstead knows. And I am asking you, as a kindness to me, to stop.

MARIA. I cannot. I am sorry. The feelings we have –

LADY COOKE. But what of your duty – your Christian duty? To behave according to your station in life, without pretensions or ambitions –

MARIA. When it was Thomas Corder you didn't care about station – you said / love will have its way...

Enter PETER.

PETER. What's going on?

LADY COOKE. Peter – I thought you were out.

PETER. Why is Maria here?

LADY COOKE. She was kind enough to pay me a visit.

PETER. Are you interfering?

LADY COOKE. I am telling her that this – whatever it is between you – this needs to end. You know it does, Peter.

PETER. I know no such thing.

LADY COOKE. What's the alternative? That you marry her?

Don't be ridiculous – Father will cut you off with nothing. You can't live here, my husband won't allow it. He cannot be seen to support you consorting with someone... like her...

PETER. What do you mean, '*like her*'?

LADY COOKE. The penniless daughter of a labourer that has already had a child with another man.

PETER. She is going to have our baby.

A beat.

LADY COOKE. Oh, you foolish girl. One accident can be forgiven, but *two* –

PETER. She did not have an accident. It's what we wanted. I will not abandon the mother of my child, Mary.

LADY COOKE. Let me speak to Miss Marten alone.

PETER. Certainly not.

MARIA. It's alright, Peter.

A beat.

PETER. I will take you home when you are ready.

He goes.

LADY COOKE. I envy you, Maria. I was betrothed to Lord Cooke at the age of sixteen and he was so rich nobody even thought to ask my opinion.

My husband is very angry with me for bringing my brother here. I do not blame you for loving him. What sort of life do you imagine that you might have together?

MARIA. We talked of a house, perhaps in Ipswich. Not too far from my family, but enough to start again. He would like to run a business, he could begin by making investments –

LADY COOKE. Invest what? My father has already written him out of his will, did you know?

MARIA *didn't know.*

My brother has never had a day without money in his life. Don't you see how this will end? With the best will in the world you cannot make him happy.

MARIA. He will never leave me. He is too good.

LADY COOKE. Which is why you must leave him. If you love him, and I think you do, then you must be the one to break it off.

LADY COOKE *goes*.

MARIA. If I had married Peter Mathews and lived a long and happy – or even unhappy – life with him, you would not be here. You would not care about that story.

PETER *comes forward. They hug tightly; he is weeping copiously.*

It's alright, my love. We will live. You will be happy.

PETER. I'll send you five pounds every three months – is that enough?

MARIA. More than enough.

PETER. And clothes, and whatever else you need. And I'll visit, of course, as often as I can. I will never love anybody else.

MARIA. I won't hold you to that.

PETER. I want you to have these.

She opens a box with some earrings inside.

They were my mother's. Please wear them, for me.

He goes.

MARIA. I wore the earrings every day until my death.

Our son Henry was born at Christmas, and I had everything I needed. A new bed for the lying-in; warm clothes, plenty of food.

But I was full of the lessons Polstead had taught me: do not dream, do not dare to hope, your position in life is given by God, it is not for you to change.

Most of the villagers did not speak to me, now. They told my story to their children, with a warning: 'Do not be the girl who thinks she's better than she is.' At church, the Vicar's wife refused to shake my hand.

For three years I trudged from day to day, week to week, season to season. Mud, pigs, children, repeat. Until one day I saw Thomas Corder about to walk across Polstead Pond.

Enter THOMAS *from the other side of the stage. He sees* MARIA *and starts to back away.*

MARIA. Hello, Thomas.

THOMAS. Miss Marten…

MARIA. I hear it is your birthday? I just wanted to wish you many happy returns.

THOMAS. Thank you. Ah – please excuse me –

MARIA. Can we still not have a polite conversation, Thomas?

THOMAS. Ah – there's Reverend Whitmore – please excuse me, I have an urgent matter to discuss –

He starts to cross the ice.

MARIA. Be careful of the ice…

THOMAS. No, no, it's quite safe.

Reverend Whitmore?

The ice cracks. THOMAS *wobbles.*

Oh…

MARIA. Are you alright?

The ice cracks loudly, and THOMAS *falls through.*

Help! Help – he's fallen in!

The company rushes forward and, with ad-libbing if required, carefully drag THOMAS *out. But by the time they get his body to the side of the pond, he is already dead.*

Thomas Corder's death was a terrible shock to his family.

His mother called her next son home from London to manage the farm. His name was William Corder. From the moment we laid eyes on each other, we were hooked. A fairytale romance.

Two years later, after hitting me with the green umbrella, William Corder pulled this earring out of my ear, and then shot me once through the neck with a pistol.

He walked across the field to the house of my friend Phoebe Stowe and asked if he could borrow her spade.

When he came back he realised I was still breathing, so he hit me many times with the spade, until I really, definitely, was dead. Then he buried me under the floor of the barn before walking away.

My flesh has rotted away, so much of this will never be known. I am just a guilty collection of clothes and bones. Waiting to be found by someone that loves me.

Enter ANN. *She is in her nightgown, her hair everywhere, crying and muttering. She looks half-crazed.*

ANN. Maria! Maria!

She staggers about the barn.

Enter PHOEBE.

PHOEBE. Ann! This has to stop – it's the middle of the night.

ANN. She's here. I know it. I saw it.

PHOEBE. You didn't see it, Annie, we've been over this so many times.

ANN. No, no –

PHOEBE. She's in the Isle of Wight, she's moved on.

ANN. No, no, no, I dreamt it again –

PHOEBE. What?

ANN. She's here, God is telling me in my dreams – God is telling me that she's here…

ANN wanders around the barn, moving hay bales.

PHOEBE. What are you talking about? Don't lift those – they're heavy –

With almost superhuman strength, ANN moves a hay bale on her own.

Behind it is the green umbrella. Tattered and broken.

ANN picks it up. They both stare at it in horror.

Oh, God.

ANN. She's here.

For a moment they are paralysed with fear.

Then PHOEBE is galvanised into action.

PHOEBE. I'll get men with torches and the constable. We need witnesses. No one will believe us.

Annie… don't…

But ANN has found a patch of floor with a few loose stones.

She scrabbles frantically with her bare hands.

And then she lifts a stone.

She looks underneath it.

ANN. Oh. Ohh.

PHOEBE joins her and looks into the hole.

She crosses herself and puts her arm around ANN.

PHOEBE. It's alright.

You've found her.

ANN sobs over the hole in the floor, while PHOEBE comforts her.

And then blackout.

ACT TWO

MARIA. I'm in the Corder's farmhouse at the bottom of the hill. Standing in the kitchen with Lucy, who has just started work there as a housemaid.

Out of the corner of my eye, I can see him in the corridor. Dark hair, quite short. His face is in shadow. I can't read his expression, but I think he's trying not to laugh.

Nobody knows yet, you see.

Nobody else has heard what he whispers when we're alone, the promises he makes, the tears of passion and delight. I wish you could all experience this joy, just once in your lives, and then you would understand how real love sounds.

This is it, and it makes the past worthwhile.

* * *

LUCY *comes forward.*

LUCY. You were definitely flirting.

MARIA. That wasn't flirting, that was just warming up. D'you want him yourself?

LUCY. William Corder is my employer. I am his mother's servant.

MARIA. He's handsome though?

LUCY. Maria!

MARIA. I'm sorry, I just can't resist the magnetic power I have over young men.

LUCY. It's not funny.

MARIA. Is it because you don't want me walking out with your master?

LUCY. He stares. At me.

MARIA. Lucy Baalham, you are a beautiful young woman, of course he stares. He's a man.

LUCY. You never listen to what I say.

I have to go. There'll be gleaning at dawn.

* * *

MARIA. The morning is crispy and pink and he's there, waiting for me in the field. He says 'you're late' and I say 'you missed me' and he kisses me hard.

I can see the others arriving with their baskets, but we hide from them in the barn. His fingers run down the small of my back and I feel the triumph, like a white light under my skin. He owns this field. He owns them. And he wants me.

Music.

SARAH, THERESA, PHOEBE *and* LUCY *are gleaning. They spend most of their time bent double, picking up bits of wheat from the field. It is very uncomfortable work, and every so often* SARAH, *who is pregnant again, stretches out her back.*

PHOEBE *has a baby in a rush basket placed nearby.*

For a while they work in silence.

THERESA *stands up for a moment, gazing across the field.*

THERESA. Is that Maria and William Corder?

PHOEBE. Yeah.

THERESA. It's like they're actually eating each other's tongues.

SARAH. Unless he's got a marrow stuck down his trousers I'd say he's rather enjoying himself.

They stare at the couple, frowning, until they see MARIA *turn around suddenly. They wave, slightly sheepish. Then* MARIA *arrives, flushed with happiness. She goes straight to* PHOEBE's *baby.*

MARIA. Hello, everyone! (*Softly to the baby.*) And you, my little one! Hello!

PHOEBE. You look like you're having fun.

MARIA. I love them when they're this age. Makes me wish Henry was a baby all over again.

THERESA. She meant with Mr Corder.

MARIA. William?

PHOEBE. How long's that been going on?

MARIA. Several months.

PHOEBE. What does his mother say?

MARIA. He's too afraid to tell her. It does make me laugh – these big bold men that are completely terrified of their mothers.

THERESA. That's why your hair's different.

MARIA. Oh – I know – he likes it like this, so –

THERESA. It's a bit smart, for working in a field.

MARIA. I'm not actually, I'm going straight home. I've got to… er… (*She gestures vaguely.*)

SARAH. Dangle his carrot?

PHOEBE. You look lovely, Maria. Why don't you come with us, we're going to my house?

MARIA. I can't – he's waiting for me.

PHOEBE. Tell him not to.

A beat.

MARIA. Another day, maybe.

SARAH. He's not gonna be like the others, I hope? Get what he wants, then change his mind and break your heart?

MARIA. See you later.

She goes. There is a moment of silence as they watch her go.

PHOEBE. It's a good thing, right? That she's happy, an' all?

THERESA. Yeah.

SARAH. *Someone's* happy, at any rate.

They gaze after her, all of them unsettled and unable to quite explain why. Except for LUCY, *who is still working.*

LUCY. Is everyone else done? Because I'm happy to take the rest.

* * *

MARIA. A few days later, I meet him in the barn and I think, alright then, let's see.

So I tell him I want to break it off. That although I like him very much, I cannot risk my reputation a third time. Polstead is just too hard, there is no starting again here.

I say: you are an important man, now. You should be looking for a wife that is more suitable for your station, and out of kindness, you should let me go.

He starts to cry. I've never seen anything like it. He is saying 'no, no, no' and before I can stop him, he is down on one knee asking me to be his wife.

When I hesitate, he says that if I refuse he'll drown himself in Polstead Pond, just like his poor brother. So I say yes, because everybody loves that pond, and he laughs with joy. This passion he feels, this can surely happen only once in a lifetime?

Then we tear each other's clothes away from our bodies and there is nothing else in the world except him and me, over and over again.

Afterwards, he says, can you lend me any money, Maria? And it makes me laugh that he should be thinking of such a little thing at a time like this, but I don't care. Of course I will.

* * *

MARIA. William's going to buy a new threshing machine.

ANN. A *threshing* machine?

MARIA. It will save him a lot of money.

ANN. But then there'll be no work for any of our boys.

MARIA. He knows what he's doing.

ANN. World's changing so fast. Machinery everywhere, railroads, lighting on the street.

MARIA. It's called progress, Ann. It's exciting.

ANN. We're all going to get left behind. How's he going to pay for it, anyway?

MARIA. I'm helping him with the deposit.

ANN. You are?

MARIA. Yeah, course.

ANN. How much?

MARIA. A few pounds.

ANN. Where are you going to get that?

MARIA. From Peter's money. It hasn't arrived yet, but when it does I'll see if there's anything left over.

ANN. It's unlike Mr Mathews to be late.

MARIA. William suggested I go up to Polstead Hall and ask when it's going to arrive.

ANN. Right.

MARIA. He's always looking out for me.

ANN. That's nice.

You're getting on well with him still, then?

MARIA. Yes, I am – What d'you mean by that?

ANN. Nothing.

* * *

MARIA *and* LADY COOKE *in Polstead Hall.*

LADY COOKE. Maria.

MARIA. Thank you for seeing me, Lady Cooke.

LADY COOKE. It's about the five pounds that has gone missing?

MARIA. Yes.

LADY COOKE. Tell me again how you normally receive it.

MARIA. Peter sends a cheque for Henry every three months. I take it to the bank in Hadleigh.

LADY COOKE. Only this time...?

MARIA. It never came. I'm sure he just forgot to send it, only I thought I should check.

LADY COOKE. It's a very odd case.

MARIA. You found it?

LADY COOKE. I went to the bank – the cheque was cashed as usual.

MARIA. What? But I didn't.

LADY COOKE. I know.

MARIA. Who did, then?

LADY COOKE. How is your relationship with William Corder going?

MARIA. I'm not sure if it's right for me to discuss it with you, Lady Cooke.

LADY COOKE. Oh – you need not worry on that score. My brother is engaged.

MARIA. He is?

LADY COOKE. A Miss Harriet Hone. She's charming.

MARIA. I'm glad.

LADY COOKE. So you need have no qualms. And Mr Corder?

MARIA. We are going to be married.

LADY COOKE. Good. I'm pleased to hear it. In that case there is no problem with your five pounds, though why he didn't tell you, I have no idea.

MARIA. Tell me what?

LADY COOKE. He cashed in the cheque.

A beat.

MARIA. William did?

At the bank?

LADY COOKE. It's very strange that he didn't mention it to you.

MARIA. Um – well – he did. I just, I forgot.

She goes.

LADY COOKE. Maria? –

* * *

MARIA. I ask him straight out when I see him. It's a mistake, of course. But I need to understand why he told me to ask for my money, when he had it all along.

He simply says: 'I didn't.'

I'm so confused: he did. He *did*. He tells me I misunderstood. And now if I accuse him of theft, he could be sent to the gallows – is that what I want?

'No, no, of course not.'

Then he shouts at me for an hour. My 'sorries' are ripped viciously in half, so I stop speaking. Sometimes his face is so close to mine I can see pockmarks clogged with dirt from the field. It goes on and on. I'm exhausted, but he's standing in front of the door, so I can't leave.

In my head I go back to Harwich, and listen to the sea.

Finally he wears himself out, and sinks down into his chair. I offer to take his boots off but he kicks his feet away and tells me to get out of his sight. As I creep out of the room, I find myself wishing I could walk away and never come back.

But my body has already told me that I am late. Far too late.

* * *

LUCY *comes forward.*

LUCY. I've just been sacked.

MARIA. Why?

LUCY. Mrs Corder found out about you two, and that I knew
and didn't tell her. She says I'm disloyal.

MARIA. Oh, no – that's awful – she can't do it! I'll speak to
William –

LUCY. Did you ever stop to think what this would be like for
me? Being told by him that one day you could be my
mistress?

Or is that what you wanted? For me to call you Madam, and
curtsy to you and keep my eyes respectfully lowered while
you are speaking? Would you be like her, and give me a slap
every now and then if I make a mistake, just to keep me on
my toes?

MARIA. Lucy…

LUCY. I dreaded it, hearing about your engagement. I thought, I
do not know how I can be the servant of someone I used to
think was my friend.

Well now, I won't have to. I can just spend my time worrying
about how my mother and I are going to survive the winter.

MARIA. The thing is – I can't leave him –

LUCY. Then good luck to you both, but you're on your own.

MARIA. I think I'm in trouble –

LUCY. So what? Do you ever stop to think about the trouble
you're causing?

LUCY *goes.*

MARIA *is left alone.*

* * *

MARIA. In his presence I become a shadow, trying to take up
less and less space.

Perhaps, if I can pluck up the courage to tell him, he will be who he was again – fatherhood can change a man. So I arrange to meet with Sarah because she'll know what to say, and she promises to call round. But instead he is there, pacing up and down, speaking of money and the land and the machinery he is buying. I mention that I am due to see Sarah, and he says – 'You can't be, I saw her going off in a fine coach with Theresa and Lady Cooke.'

Lady Cooke?

'On a trip to Colchester,' he says. To see the ballet.

Of all the things I have ever longed for – and they knew that! – to go without me! When I cry he holds me and is very kind and dries my tears with his sleeve, and says he will be all the friends I need, from now on.

He stays for supper, he's charming to Ann and Father, and it's just like the old times. Later we sleep together in my childhood bed, while everyone else pretends not to notice that we have disappeared upstairs.

Just before we drift off to sleep in each other's arms, he murmurs in my ear, 'Just no babies, Maria. Not right now, with the farm…'

He strokes my face so gently, he loves me so much.

'I'm trusting you,' he says. 'Just on this one thing.'

* * *

SARAH *is standing outside her house, looking for her son.*

SARAH. Charlie? Come back here. You're worse than your father! Who also came and went at precisely the wrong time.

Enter MARIA.

Maria? Hello, love!

MARIA. Why didn't you come?

SARAH. Eh?

MARIA. You said you'd come and meet me – I waited all evening.

SARAH. I left you a message – didn't you get it?

MARIA. About the ballet?

SARAH. Ballet?

MARIA. I know you went to the ballet with Lady Cooke –

SARAH. Sorry – say that again – ?

MARIA. Don't deny it –

SARAH. I think she'd rather die than take me to a ballet. I think I'd rather die than go. Who told you this? William?

MARIA. Well. He said –

SARAH. I left a message with him. I couldn't come out cos there's no one to mind the boys, but I said for you to come here.

MARIA. Oh.

SARAH. He didn't say?

MARIA. No – he did say something – maybe I misunderstood – just I got the impression that...

SARAH. That what?

MARIA. Just that you and Theresa are always so... you're always together, just the two of you.

SARAH. Cos you're always with William, not cos we don't want you, silly.

MARIA. I knew you'd tell me I was silly.

A beat, slightly tense.

SARAH. What did you want to talk about?

MARIA. It's nothing really. I wondered if you knew about some... pills?

I heard about some pills.

SARAH. Pills for what, Maria?

MARIA. For my monthly courses – they're very painful, you see – and not altogether regular, so. I thought you might know where I could get something for it.

I heard about a doctor in Ipswich, who's a lady doctor –

SARAH. Did you now?

Maria, if you have got yourself into some sort of trouble –

MARIA. No, I haven't –

SARAH. Then there is no shame in that – look at me, I'm living my life as brazen as you like, and I don't care how many types of whore they call me in Polstead, I love my children and I would never change a thing. Don't you go visiting any doctors, do you hear me? Don't you do that.

MARIA. But he said –

SARAH. What did he say?

Just as MARIA *is about to speak,* THERESA *comes towards them, from out of* SARAH*'s house.*

THERESA. Maria! How are you?

MARIA *looks at* SARAH, *hurt.*

MARIA. You could have just told me she was here and I'd have gone.

SARAH. No – no – it wasn't like that! Theresa came round unexpectedly – don't go –

But MARIA *has gone already.*

THERESA. What's the matter with her?

SARAH. She doesn't know that John kicked you out.

THERESA. Because she never asks.

SARAH. She thinks we don't want to be friends with her.

THERESA. If she keeps running off like that, she's going to be right.

* * *

MARIA. When I tell him, he doesn't speak for ages. Then he walks out, and I don't see him for seven days.

Seven days is so long I can feel a sort of wilderness growing up inside me – *everybody leaves*. I am so utterly unlovable and disgraced.

In the end, I go to the farmhouse and ring the front doorbell, shaking from head to foot. When he answers, he pulls me into the house before anybody else can see, and drags me into a side room.

I've planned this. I kneel at his feet and kiss his shoes.

He lets the moment hang. I don't even dare to look up.

Then he steps away. I wish that I wasn't crying, that I could summon some sort of dignity. At the door he gives instructions. He tells me what to do, and what to tell everybody else that I am doing, and the two are not the same thing.

He is gone, and I vomit. I walk away and leave it there, a tiny puddle of revenge. But when I reach the kitchen I go back, and clear it up.

* * *

MARIA *and* ANN, *doing the weekly wash. It's a rigorous, exhausting, messy business, involving a lot of scrubbing and cold, dirty water. This is a whites wash.*

ANN. So you're going to stay in Sudbury for a few weeks. Just visiting a friend.

In Sudbury.

MARIA. Are you trying to make a point?

ANN. No. Nothing wrong with making a nice visit. I often go to visit friends in nearby towns and stay there for several weeks. It's a nice, sociable sort of thing. To visit.

MARIA. Exactly.

ANN. And he's gonna go too, is he? Or not?

MARIA. William is going to escort me there on his horse. And then he will come to visit, I expect.

ANN. Right. He'll visit you, visiting.

MARIA. Stop saying that.

A pause. They continue scrubbing.

ANN. When I was at Manor Farm, we all used to have to help on wash day. Bloody nightmare, it was. Started at four in the morning. Had to do all the master and missus first, then the children, then all the other servants and finally our own. Never finished before midnight.

I think you get to know someone when you wash their clothes. Can't have secrets, can you? Specially if it's a woman. One of the scullery maids had been carrying on with a farmhand, and she got into the family way and tried to keep it a secret, but we all knew because of her washing, you see? No monthly courses. We never told anyone until she got found out – and she was dismissed, of course. Terrible cruel. She had to go to the workhouse in Assington.

If there is anything you'd like to tell me, I am all ears.

I am ears only.

MARIA *just keeps working.*

Perhaps I could come and see you in Sudbury?

MARIA *shakes her head.*

Maria?

* * *

MARIA. In Sudbury I live in one room.

He could not afford a midwife, he said I must manage on my own.

There's a lot of pain, but I have done this twice before. Later I notice red streaks on the wall, which I suppose I did. The baby is small and slippery in my arms. We are joined together, we breathe in the same rhythm. She feeds, but not enough. We slip in and out of sleep for days. Sometimes she watches me, unblinking and a little sad.

I pray that I won't let her down.

* * *

PHOEBE *and* SARAH *in Sudbury.*

SARAH. This is definitely the place?

PHOEBE. That's what he said.

SARAH. Poky little street, ain't it?

PHOEBE. Never liked Sudbury much.

SARAH. Never liked *him* much. Pretending he couldn't remember the address. Why wouldn't he just give us the house number? Weaselly little man.

PHOEBE. Shall we knock at every door until we find her?

SARAH. Yeah, if you want to take all day. (*Suddenly yelling very loudly.*) Maria! It's us! *Maria*, are you there?

PHOEBE. Maybe she doesn't want to come out –

SARAH. Tell us where y'are or I'll shout your full name!

PHOEBE. There!

From the side of the stage, MARIA *enters. She's half-hidden in a blanket.*

Maria!

MARIA (*a half-whisper*). What are you doing here?

PHOEBE. We've come to see you –

MARIA. You can't, you have to go. He could arrive at any moment.

PHOEBE. William? He knows we're here – we asked him for the address.

MARIA. That was good of him.

PHOEBE. Was it?

MARIA. That gives me hope. He's very upset at the moment – it's difficult for him.

SARAH. For him, really?

MARIA. Yes – it is –

SARAH. Because in my experience, childbirth is much the harder for the woman.

MARIA. Shhhh. Don't – for God's sake –

PHOEBE. Can we come in?

MARIA. No. No – I'm afraid not, he might come today.

PHOEBE. You have had a baby, haven't you, Maria?

MARIA *nods.*

Where is it?

MARIA. Sleeping.

PHOEBE. What's happened, is it alright?

MARIA. There are. She –

Has bruises.

SARAH. Bruises?

MARIA. You should go. Please.

PHOEBE *grabs her as she starts to walk away.*

PHOEBE. We're not going – we're worried about you.

MARIA. Get off – you'll take her from me.

PHOEBE. We won't.

MARIA. Promise you won't tell anyone –

PHOEBE. We promise, don't we, Sarah?

SARAH. Yeah.

A beat.

MARIA. I gave them to her. The bruises.

PHOEBE. You hurt her?

MARIA. I was so tired. I fell asleep, and when I woke William was there, shaking me, and shouting – he was in a terrible state, and the baby was screaming.

He said I'd hurt her. He'd walked into the room, and as he entered he saw me.

And then he said –

There are strangle marks.

Do you think I'll be locked away? Is there a devil in me?

PHOEBE. Where is William now?

MARIA. He was so angry and upset – he left and hasn't come back.

SARAH. How long ago was this?

MARIA. I don't know, I lost count of the days.

PHOEBE. When did you last go to sleep?

MARIA. I can't close my eyes, in case I do it again. I don't even want to blink.

PHOEBE. Listen to me, Maria, apart from that moment, has she suffered from any other mysterious injuries?

MARIA. No.

PHOEBE. Do you want to harm your baby?

MARIA. I don't seem to have control over what I do – and William hates me now, because I am a bad mother –

PHOEBE. Do you think there could be any other explanation for the bruises?

MARIA. No – he saw it happen.

SARAH (*to* PHOEBE). We should take her home –

MARIA. I can't leave here – this is the only place he knows where to find us.

PHOEBE. Right, love. This is what we'll do. We'll come in –

MARIA. No – no –

PHOEBE. – Just to see the baby? And then why don't we look after her while you have a wash, get you ready to see William in case he visits?

MARIA. He might like that.

PHOEBE. And then, if he don't come at all, how about we take you home to your father's?

MARIA. No one must know about the child. It's a secret.

A beat.

PHOEBE. Why, love?

MARIA. He doesn't want anyone to know.

SARAH. Everyone's going to find out eventually.

MARIA. But I promised him – he'll be angry –

PHOEBE. Alright, we'll keep it a secret.

SARAH. I'll pretend I've 'ad another one, shall I? No one'll bat an eyelid.

PHOEBE. Come on, let's get you put right.

Music.

Tenderly they wash MARIA *and change her clothes.*
SARAH *fetches a basket with the baby in and checks that it is sleeping.*

At one point MARIA *tries to speak to the audience.*

But she cannot find any words.

They help her offstage.

* * *

PHOEBE *and* ANN *in the Martens' cottage.*

ANN. Thank you for bringing her home.

PHOEBE. How is she?

ANN. I dunno. I tried to talk to her a couple of times. I tell you, I've seen a few bad men in my day, and he's one of 'em. I don't like it.

PHOEBE. Does he visit them?

ANN. Yeah. He shouted at her for telling us about the baby, we heard it all. Then he goes out the back without saying a word. And she comes down afterwards saying how kind and good he is, and how we don't make him feel welcome.

Her father nearly came to blows with him last week. Asked him to his face when the marriage was going to happen. Baby's six weeks old now, he should be making an honest woman of her.

MARIA *enters*.

Maria?

PHOEBE. How are you?

MARIA. I did it, I finally killed her and she is dead.

ANN. What?

PHOEBE. The baby? Where is she?

ANN. Go and look.

PHOEBE *goes*.

MARIA. She's not there, William took her because he saw me do it. He saw me hurt her, without even knowing. You should stay away in case I hurt you too.

ANN. Oh, God save us –

MARIA. Think about it, Annie. I could not be a mother to a *girl*. What sort of example would I be?

ANN. Maria, where has he taken her? Where has he gone?

MARIA. To the field. To pray, I expect. For a better mother to his child next time.

Enter PHOEBE. *She shakes her head at* ANN.

They will come for me soon. This is two girls now that I have lost, it cannot be a coincidence. There'll be a constable, perhaps even soldiers.

PHOEBE. Maria, take a hold of yourself, there will be no constable. Think of little Henry, he needs you, remember?

MARIA. Yes, but Henry will be fine. He is brave and can fight me back if I turn on him.

ANN. You didn't do this, Maria. You would never hurt your own child. If she is gone, it is because God took her, not because of you.

MARIA. But the evidence was very plain.

ANN. No – not to me –

PHOEBE. I think William must have made a mistake – don't you? In his grief.

MARIA. His grief. Do you think so?

ANN. Remember she was very sick? Over the last few days – she had a fever, don't you remember?

MARIA. Yes... she did.

ANN. And you were worried about her, we all were.

MARIA. He told me to go back to bed and pretend it never happened, because if this gets out I will be hanged.

ANN. No one will be hanged, love.

* * *

MARIA. You didn't say. Did you? You watched it all, and you never said – 'Stop it, Maria, take her and get out now, there is something very wrong here.'

You didn't say – 'If you die now, the stories they will tell about you will not be kind.' I'm not some blushing virgin they can write poems about.

But that's why you're here, of course. You've come for the dead woman and the bones under the barn. You want to watch me die – this is the bit you've all been waiting for.

You're here to see my blood. But I don't need to show you that. You've already imagined it enough times yourselves.

You won't mourn me. You're just –

Curious.

It's alright. I'd probably have done the same.

This is the end of the story, for me. But not for them. After this, I will disappear for a whole year while the world carries on just the same. Summer, autumn, winter, spring, until my stepmother will dig up my bones with her bare hands and then my friends will fall apart with grief.

In fact, the worst bit isn't my death. The worst is how I said goodbye.

* * *

The Martens' cottage. ANN *finds* MARIA *hiding.*

ANN. Maria? What are you doing?

MARIA. They're after me – they're coming up the hill –

ANN. Who is?

MARIA. Shhh – the constable – they're going to arrest me –

ANN. What for?

MARIA. For burdening the parish with too many bastards and for killing my little girl. There are too many bastards, Ann –

ANN. Hush, this is silly – who told you this?

MARIA. William came back! It's a miracle – he came back and told me he loves me – can you believe him? But there's a warrant out for my arrest. I'll be sent to Australia and poor little Henry will have no one –

ANN. Stop this –

MARIA. So he's going to take me away. I need to be in disguise.

She starts to take off her clothes.

ANN. What?

MARIA. If I go as a man, they will not know me and I will not be stopped.

ANN. Maria! Stop it!

The ensemble come forward to help MARIA *change into a man's shirt and breeches. She is confused and then angered by their help, finally pushing them violently away.*

MARIA. *No.*

Shhhhh. It's alright. It's alright. They won't know it's me.

ANN. Maria...

MARIA *finishes changing. For a moment she is still.*

What is it, love? What's happened to you?

MARIA (*a whisper*). I don't know.

I think I must be a very wicked person.

ANN. No. No, love. You never were wicked in your life.

MARIA. I can't seem to work out what's right.

ANN. I don't think anybody's coming after you.

MARIA. But William saw them.

ANN. I think he must be wrong.

MARIA. He is the only one who ever truly loved me, though sometimes I doubt him, and then he gets so upset.

ANN. Maria. Has William ever hurt you? Or the baby, perhaps? Did he ever hit you?

MARIA. You see? This is what happens when you doubt someone who's good. *No.* No, no, no, no, no. He has never laid a finger on me. In all the trouble, in all my life, he is the only one who has ever really wanted me, even though I'm a bad mother.

ANN. You are not a –

MARIA. He wants it to be just us. Isn't that the most beautiful thing you ever heard?

He wants me all to himself, far away from all this, far away from Polstead. You see, I have relied on friends and family like a child. Oh, I don't deserve him, he is right. But now, I shall show him I need no one else, I am going to go with him and make him happy.

ANN. What man wants a woman he loves to have no friends?

MARIA. It's just his way. He loves me so much, you see? He's prepared to risk his life for my sake.

She starts to move around the space, picking up things. She puts her earrings on. She ties the green handkerchief around her neck. She picks up the green umbrella.

She looks very odd.

ANN. Don't say goodbye like this.

MARIA. I will send for Henry when we reach the Isle of Wight.

ANN. The Isle of *Wight*?

MARIA. That's where we'll be married, and safe. I will write to you.

ANN. I don't trust him.

MARIA. If anything happens it will be your fault! You never gave him a chance. It's no wonder he wants to get me away from you.

ANN. Maria! –

MARIA. He's the only one that really loves me – and yet you hate him! You talk about him behind his back – you're always insinuating that I should give him up. It just makes me love him all the more – I will never forget what you have done to us – I hate you!

A knock on the door.

ANN (*looking out of the window*). It's William.

MARIA. Oh! Thank goodness! You see? What a good man he is!

ANN. He's gone again.

MARIA. I'm to meet him at the red barn. I have to go.

ANN. Please don't. Stay and we'll talk –

MARIA. When the officers come looking for me, try to put them off the scent, will you, Ann? Tell them we have gone to Norwich. Or Wales, or something –

ANN. Please –

MARIA. I won't say goodbye to Henry, I can't bear it. But tell him, it won't be for long.

And MARIA *goes.*

* * *

PHOEBE *is outside her own cottage.*

PHOEBE. Hello?

William Corder approaches her, unseen.

Oh. Hello, Mr Corder. Yes, sir, it's a lovely day. How's Maria?

A spade? Course. There's one in the vegetable patch – I'll get it for you now.

Alright – help yourself, if you're in such a hurry.

Bye, then.

Blackout.

ACT THREE

One year later. SARAH, PHOEBE, ANN *and* THERESA.

SARAH. They found him.

PHOEBE. Where?

SARAH. London. He was living at a girls' school. Married the teacher.

PHOEBE. *Married?* When?

SARAH. Last autumn.

ANN. But that's only just after Maria left. Whole year's gone by, and she was in the barn all that time.

SARAH. He placed an advertisement in the newspaper, 'a grieving widower looking for love and companionship'.

PHOEBE. Who would respond to that?

SARAH. About a hundred women, apparently. She's expecting his child while he goes on trial for murder.

ANN. A trial?

SARAH. It's a good thing. He'll hang.

ANN. I'll have to speak, won't I?

PHOEBE. I expect so. You're a witness – you'll have to tell them how you found the body.

SARAH. Wish I could be a witness. Send the bastard to hell.

THERESA. We don't know he did it.

A beat.

PHOEBE. What?

THERESA. John says he would never hurt anyone.

PHOEBE. And obviously, John knows best.

THERESA. He's known him all his life. It's been very hard for him.

PHOEBE. Being friends with a murderer? Yeah, must be terrible. Poor, drunk John.

SARAH. Not now, Phoebe.

THERESA. Yes, not now, *Phoebe*. We can't all be blessed with angels like your Francis.

PHOEBE. Thing is, I don't have very much sympathy with violent men, probably because two weeks ago, I found my best friend's dead body buried in a barn. And your husband is going around the village saying she killed herself.

THERESA. She might have. She was a mess at the end – always crying and running off. Wouldn't put it past her.

PHOEBE. Take that back.

THERESA. I'm just saying, nobody knows.

PHOEBE. Strangled herself, did she? With the handkerchief *we* gave her? You're half the woman she was –

THERESA. Well I certainly only slept with half the men.

PHOEBE. Not for want of trying, though –

ANN. *Stop it*. Have some respect.

She loved you all – don't tear yourselves up because of her.

* * *

LUCY *is sitting on a bench.*

PHOEBE *approaches and sits with her.*

PHOEBE. You didn't go to the trial today, then?

Me neither.

LUCY. I'm trying to remember what she looked like. I can't see her face.

PHOEBE. That's what death does. I like to remember the dancing. The Cherry Fair?

LUCY. I do not wish to be comforted by you.

PHOEBE. Me?

LUCY. Yes. No. Not by you.

PHOEBE. I just caught sight of you from my window, that's why I came. To see if you were alright.

LUCY. You never asked before. None of you ever did.

PHOEBE. Right then. (*Standing.*) I'll be on my way.

LUCY. You saw her body. You saw the bones, and the skull.

You gave him the spade.

A beat.

PHOEBE. Yeah.

LUCY. How can you bear it? How are you even breathing? I can barely stand under the weight of it, and yet you do, and you go on with your husband and your children as if the world did not contain her in the first place.

PHOEBE. Lucy, come into the house? I'll put the kettle on –

LUCY. Yes – that's it. A man is on trial as we speak, in front of a crowd of thousands, for horribly murdering our friend, and you make tea.

PHOEBE. My grief is not your business.

LUCY. I do not see your grief – I don't / see any –

PHOEBE. Well you weren't looking, were you? You didn't help her, at the end. You told her you didn't want to see her again – we all knew that.

LUCY. Of course I didn't – she was –

PHOEBE. She was *what*?

Winning?

There was a game between you two, and she didn't even know she was in it, did she? The game of winning the rich farmer. What happened?

I'm not even sure I want to know.

LUCY. No one ever liked me. I'm not fun, am I? Not witty, or clever, I don't wear nice clothes. I don't even have friends, really – and don't pretend you're all my friends because I know you're not. You're just honouring the memory of what we were.

William used to talk to me late into the night about the farm and his worries for the harvest. He was kind.

I began to notice he was different around me. He'd drop something and when I bent to pick it up he would be staring. If we passed in a narrow corridor he would press up close. One day in the parlour he grabbed my hand and said he couldn't stop thinking about me. He said he was going to finish with Maria and marry me. We kissed.

And then I let him...

I thought it was a miracle – this tidal wave of joy.

I went home and told Mother – she wept with delight to think of a wedding. It was the first and only time I have ever made her proud. We spent the whole night planning the future. In the morning I packed a bag and took it to work.

And he behaved as if nothing had happened. He gave commands, he worked, he didn't look me in the eye. When I tried to speak to him, he said he had no idea what I was talking about. He said it with such confidence that I began to think him right.

Mother said I had imagined the whole thing.

Truth is, he didn't care for me.

He didn't even care enough to kill me.

PHOEBE. Lucy –

LUCY. I know. I disgust myself.

PHOEBE. He was a devil – he *made* you feel like that.

LUCY. If he was the devil, I was tempted, and I fell.

I have to give evidence at the trial.

PHOEBE. I know – I do too, I have to go and talk about the spade. It's going to be horrible but I keep thinking: I have some power here. We can help to send him down.

LUCY. For the defence.

PHOEBE. What?

LUCY. I'm one of his character witnesses.

PHOEBE. What are you going to do?

LUCY. I don't have any choice. I have to go and tell the truth.

PHOEBE. Tell them what he did to you –

LUCY. Nobody in their right minds would believe he proposed to *me*. He was my employer, and he never gave me a cross word.

PHOEBE. Don't stick up for him –

LUCY. 'He always behaved like a kind and good-natured man.' That's what his lawyer has told me to say.

PHOEBE. If you say that, I will not speak to you again, Lucy Baalham.

LUCY. But / what –

PHOEBE. Think of something. For all your stupid posturing about not being clever, that head of yours works as well as mine.

We all know he did it. Don't let him walk away.

* * *

SARAH *and* THERESA. THERESA *has her back to* SARAH.

SARAH. You can't do it, Theresa – you can't defend him.

THERESA. I don't have a choice.

SARAH. He took her to Sudbury – he hit the baby and made her think she'd done it – he stole from her –

THERESA. I wasn't there for any of that – you went with Phoebe, not me –

SARAH. But I'm telling you it happened.

THERESA. And I'm telling you I wasn't there.

She turns round. She has a large bruise on her face.

SARAH. Bastard's hit you again.

THERESA. No – we had a row.

SARAH. I can see that.

THERESA. He's told me what to say: 'He was a kind, good-tempered and humane man.'

SARAH. Ignore what John says –

THERESA. I swore in a church to love and obey him for the rest of my life – I promised.

SARAH. Don't you understand: John is just the same? Maybe you'll be dead next – had you thought of that?

THERESA. That's ridiculous!

SARAH. I wish it was – I really do – Theresa!

But THERESA *has gone.*

* * *

THERESA, LUCY *and* ANN *are giving evidence at the trial.*

ANN. She was dressed as a man, because he told her she was going to be arrested.

An earring is passed to her.

These are her earrings.

The umbrella is passed to her.

That's –

That's her umbrella.

She goes.

THERESA *steps into the light.*

THERESA. He was a kind, good tempered and humane man.

She goes.

LUCY *steps into the spotlight.*

LUCY. He always behaved like a kind and good-natured man.

A beat. Then suddenly –

Wait. I saw a pair of pistols in his bedroom.

He kept two pistols, sometimes in a box. He loved them. He was always carrying them around.

The spotlight fades.

* * *

Night. In front of the red barn.

LUCY, ANN, THERESA, SARAH *and* PHOEBE.

A couple of them hold candles or lanterns. SARAH *holds a flaming torch.*

PHOEBE. Sarah? What's going on?

THERESA. Why've you called us?

SARAH. I'm calling a meeting of the Hazard Club.

ANN. The what?

PHOEBE. It's that silly game we had when we were children.

THERESA. The Hazard Club was finished years ago.

SARAH. I'm starting it up again. (*To* ANN.) You're the newest member.

ANN. Why does it have to be in the middle of the night?

SARAH. This is an emergency.

THERESA. Is someone ill? Cos if not, I'm going back to bed.

SARAH. We are fighting for our lives here, can't you see that? Look at us! Fighting, and losing, and fighting again, and losing. Because no one will listen.

(*To* LUCY.) I saw you in court today. You tried your best – but they don't question the women properly. They keep discounting what we're saying. They spent more time questioning Theresa's bloody John than you, even though he knew nothing.

PHOEBE. He's going to be found guilty.

SARAH. How d'you know that?

PHOEBE. Because he's made too many mistakes. He lied about the spade, the pistols. He'll hang for it.

ANN. D'you think so?

SARAH. So what if he does? It's not enough, is it? He'll have the last word. The books will be written about him, not Maria. People come here like the barn is sacred and steal bits of it, like it's some sort of glorious act of love, instead of something horrible. Even her grave has been wrecked. She loved words, but no one will ever hear her.

I want us to take vengeance.

ANN. Vengeance?

LUCY. That don't sound very Christian – I'm not hurting anyone.

SARAH. We won't hurt anyone. We just need it to stop.

ANN. How?

SARAH. I want to burn it down.

PHOEBE. What?

SARAH. The barn. It's a monument to what they can do to us, over and over again. I want to burn it to the ground.

LUCY. That's *wanton* destruction of someone else's property.

SARAH. Yeah.

ANN. You can't burn down a barn!

Can you?

PHOEBE. Why not?

ANN. It won't bring her back.

SARAH. It'll feel bloody great, though.

LUCY. I'll do it.

I'll do it now.

SARAH. She always said you were brave.

LUCY. I'll do it for her.

PHOEBE. Yes!

THERESA. No, you won't. If any one of you so much as enters the barn I'll call the constable.

SARAH. Theresa – come on –

THERESA. Stop telling me what to do. I'll not stand by while you – you –

SARAH. What? Break the rules? Rules we had no say in. Always being told to be quiet and mind our place. I'm not doing that any more, I can't – I can't do it.

Go on, Lucy.

THERESA. Don't go on, Lucy –

SARAH. Let her!

THERESA. Stand back! If you come any closer I will have you all reported to the constable and accused of plotting to commit arson, and I will happily watch your miserable faces as you board the boat to Australia.

SARAH. Theresa!

THERESA. You think I won't, but I will.

SARAH. This is because of John.

THERESA. It's got nothing to do / with –

SARAH. It has everything to do with it! Your John makes up new rules all the time and then when you break them he grinds you into a pulp, and then you come round to my house and I wash the blood off your face. How long are you going to live like this, until we have to bury you as well?

LUCY *steps forward*.

LUCY. I'm going to do it.

THERESA *moves in between* LUCY *and the barn.* SARAH *steps forward with her arms out, as if to move* THERESA *out of the way, but she flinches violently. In the commotion,* LUCY *is thrown onto the ground.*

THERESA (*screaming*). Get off – get off – don't touch me!

SARAH. Alright, alright…

THERESA. Get away –

SARAH. I won't – I won't touch you.

They watch THERESA*'s overreaction, gasping and crying.*

A moment.

It's not your fault, Theresa.

It's not.

THERESA. He makes me feel like it is.

SARAH. Yeah. But he's wrong.

A beat.

THERESA. I hate him.

SARAH. What?

THERESA. I hate him.

SARAH. That's good – that's progress.

PHOEBE. Louder?

THERESA. I hate him!

PHOEBE. Yeah!

THERESA. If I ever see his face again –

SARAH. You won't have to.

THERESA. I'll punch him back –

PHOEBE. Too right!

THERESA. Punch him really hard –

SARAH. Well – maybe not *hard* –

THERESA. Punch him so hard my fist goes right through his skin and into his chest cavity and then rip out his heart and feel it pumping in my hands.

SARAH. Maybe just... come and live with me? One murder trial's probably enough for my lifetime.

THERESA. Yeah, alright.

ANN. Look! Over there at the edge of the village.

LUCY. It's my uncle and the other constable – they've seen our lights.

SARAH. We haven't got long. D'you want to?

LUCY. Will they know it was us?

PHOEBE. Not if we run straight away – we can say we were in my house all along.

LUCY. My hands are shaking.

SARAH. I'll stand with you.

PHOEBE. And me.

ANN. Me too.

They look at THERESA.

THERESA. Me too.

SARAH. Let's do it together.

She holds out her hand to LUCY. *They go forward together with her lantern.*

They set light to the straw in the barn.

At first, nothing.

And then the sound of a small crackle.

PHOEBE. It's going up.

SARAH. This is our promise. We will never be silenced again. We will stand together, and when they try to make us quiet, and behave, and give in, we will burn it all down.

Because she had a life, and she should have lived it.

The fire starts to build.

They watch the barn burn down.

Flames light their faces.

ANN. Goodbye, Maria.

Goodbye, my love.

Goodbye.

In the flickering light, MARIA *walks across the stage. She holds the green umbrella, which she puts up and holds above her head. Then she walks away.*

They stand there, together.

The lights fade to black.

The End.